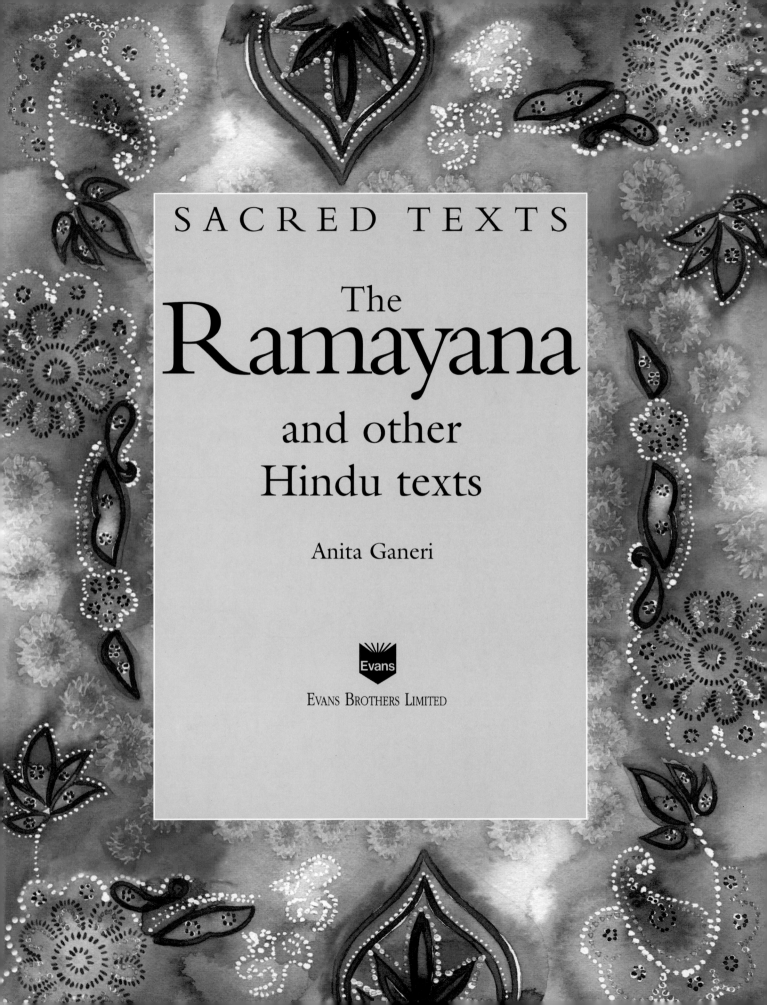

SACRED TEXTS

# The
# Ramayana
## and other
## Hindu texts

Anita Ganeri

Evans

EVANS BROTHERS LIMITED

First published in paperback in 2008 by
Evans Brothers Limited
2A Portman Mansions
Chiltern St
London W1U 6NR

Text copyright © Anita Ganeri 2003
© in the illustrations Evans Brothers Ltd 2003

British Library Cataloguing in Publication Data
Ganeri, Anita
    The Ramayana. – (Sacred texts)
    1. Ramayana 2. Hinduism – Juvenile literature
    I. Title
    294.5'922

ISBN 9780237536374

Printed in China by WKT Co. Ltd

Editors: Nicola Barber, Louise John
Designer: Simon Borrough
Illustrations: Tracy Fennell, Allied Artists
Production: Jenny Mulvanny
Consultant: Professor Gavin Flood, Department
of Religious Studies, University of Sterling

Picture acknowledgements:
Ancient Art and Architecture Collection Ltd: 8, 13t
(Dr Sheridan).
Bridgeman Art Library: 20 (Lauros / Giraudon).
Circa Photo Library: 6 (Bipin J Mistry), 7 (John
Smith), 10, 11 (William Holtby), 13b (Bipin
J Mistry), 14 (Bipin J Mistry), 16, 19b (Bipin J
Mistry), 21, 22 (John Smith), 23t (John Smith),
24 (Bipin J Mistry).
Hutchinson Library: 18 (Jeremy Horner), 25 (K
Rodgers), 26 (J G Fuller).
Trip: 9 (R Graham), 12 (Dinodia), 19t (H Rogers), 23b
(H Rogers), 27 (Dinodia).
Cover © Doranne Jacobson

To my uncle, Vishnu
Kant Shastri. A. G.

In this book dates are written
using BCE, which means 'Before
the Common Era', and CE,
which means 'in the Common
Era'. These abbreviations replace
BC (Before Christ) and AD
(Anno Domini 'in the year of
our Lord') which are based on
the Christian calendar.

The quotations in
this book have been
translated, and
adapted to suit the
age range, from
the original text
of the Ramayana
and other Hindu
sacred texts.

# Contents

In each of the world's six main religions – Hinduism, Judaism, Buddhism, Islam, Christianity and Sikhism – sacred texts play an important part. They teach people how to practise their faith and guide them throughout their lives. Wherever these books are read or studied, they are treated with great care and respect because they are so precious.

# Introduction

## Hindu sacred texts

Hindus are followers of a religion called Hinduism. The word 'Hindu' was first used by the ancient Persians to describe the people living on the eastern side of the River Indus (in modern-day Pakistan). Hindus themselves call their religion sanatana dharma, or 'eternal teaching'. For Hindus, dharma does not simply mean a set of religious rules and beliefs. It is a code of behaviour by which they live their daily lives.

## Heard and remembered

Unlike religions such as Islam and Christianity, Hinduism does not have just one holy book. Many different texts are considered sacred. These are divided into two groups, called shruti and smriti. Shruti means 'that which is heard'. It is believed that a group of wise men heard these texts directly from Brahman (God). The Vedas and Upanishads are shruti texts. Smriti means 'that which is remembered'. These later texts were composed by people, then memorised and passed on. Smriti texts include the Ramayana, the Mahabharata and the Puranas.

*Hindus bathing in the sacred River Ganges.*

*"Fortitude, forgiveness, self control, generosity, purity of mind and body, calmness, study of the scriptures, meditation on God, truthfulness, freedom from anger – this is the tenfold path of virtue."*

(MANUSMRITI: THE LAWS OF MANU)

*Priests and devotees studying
the sacred texts.*

## Using the sacred texts

Ordinary Hindus do not usually read the shruti texts
straight through. They learn the prayers used in daily
worship by heart. Priests recite verses from the texts in
the mandir, or temple, and on special occasions, such as
a baby's naming ceremony or a wedding. The smriti
texts are much more popular with most Hindus and
are read by millions of people every day. The stories in
the texts teach important values, such as love, duty and
loyalty.

## Hinduism today

Today, there are about 700 million Hindus. About two
thirds of Hindus still live in India, where Hinduism
began. But there are Hindu communities all over the
world, especially in countries such as Britain, the USA
and Canada. Wherever Hindus have settled, their
Hindu dharma, as set out in the sacred texts, is very
important to them.

# Origins

## How Hinduism began

Hinduism is the world's oldest religion, but there is no set date for when it began. Its origins go back about 4500 years, to the time of the Indus Valley civilisation. This highly developed society flourished from about 2500 BCE to 1500 BCE along the banks of the River Indus in northwest India (modern-day Pakistan).

## The Indus Valley

Indus Valley culture centred around the two great cities of Harappa and Mohenjo Daro. The cities were laid out in a grid pattern and divided into two parts – the lower town where most people lived, and a hilltop fort, or citadel, used as a government and religious centre.

Many clay figures have been found among the ruins of the Indus cities. A lot of these figures are in the form of a goddess, similar to the mother goddess in later Hinduism. She was worshipped as a goddess of life and creation.

Among the artefacts found at the Indus sites are hundreds of small, stone seals. These seals were used by merchants to mark their goods. Some show animals, such as bulls and elephants. Others show religious scenes. Each seal has an inscription but no one has yet been able to decode the Indus script.

# The Vedic period

Some scholars believe that, in about 1500 BCE, groups of Aryan people from Central Asia began to arrive in northwest India. They brought with them their own religion, which mixed with the religion of the Indus Valley to form the basis of Hinduism. The time of the Aryans is called the Vedic period, after their religious beliefs which were later written down as the Vedas (see pages 12-13).

## Vedic religion

The Aryans worshipped many gods, especially those connected with nature. The most important were Agni, god of fire, Varuna, keeper of order in the universe and Indra, god of war, the sky, storms and rain. The Aryans offered sacrifices to the gods to gain their favour. As the priests performed the sacrifices, they sang hymns and prayers in praise of the gods. These hymns make up the Rig Veda, one of the most sacred Hindu texts (see pages 12-13).

"Let me now sing the great deeds of Indra, the wielder of the thunderbolt. He killed the Great Serpent, set the rivers free and broke down the mountain barriers." (RIG VEDA)

*The ruins of Mohenjo Daro, one of the great Indus cities.*

# What Hindus believe

Hinduism is a very varied and flexible religion. There are many different ways of being a Hindu and of worshipping. But most Hindus share the same basic beliefs and values. These are set out in the sacred texts. Hindus try to behave according to the dharma, which means doing their duty towards their family, working hard and telling the truth.

## God and the soul

Most Hindus believe in a great soul or spirit, called Brahman. Brahman is the all-powerful, eternal force behind all existence. Some Hindus worship Brahman as God. Other Hindus think that Brahman is a great power beyond all description. Hinduism also teaches that every living thing has an individual soul, called atman, which lives on after the body has died.

> "From the unreal
>     lead me to the real.
> From the darkness
>     lead me to the light.
> From death
>     lead me to immortality."
> (BRIHADARANYAKA UPANISHAD)

*A shrine to Rama, the Hindu god, and his wife Sita.*

## Gods and goddesses

In Hinduism, people worship God in many forms. There are hundreds of gods and goddesses. Hindus believe that each of these deities is a way of expressing a different aspect of Brahman's power. The three most important Hindu gods are Brahma, the

*A holy man worshipping on the banks of the River Ganges.*

There are four paths that Hindus can follow to reach moksha. They can choose the path that suits them best.

1. Bhakti yoga – the path of loving devotion to God.
2. Karma yoga – the path of good, selfless actions.
3. Jnana yoga – the path of knowledge and study of the sacred texts.
4. Raja yoga – the path of yoga and meditation.

creator of the universe; Vishnu, the protector; and Shiva, the destroyer. The other most popular deities are Rama and Krishna, two avatars, or forms, of Vishnu; Ganesha, the elephant-headed god; and Shakti, the great goddess. Hindus do not worship all the deities. Many have a favourite god or goddess who is special to their family.

## Life and death

Hindus believe that, when you die, your atman, or soul, is reborn in another body. This can happen again and again. This cycle of birth, death and rebirth is called samsara. The quality of your next life depends on how you behave in this one. Good actions bring a higher rebirth. Bad actions bring a lower one. This is called karma. The aim of a Hindu's life is to escape from samsara and reach moksha, or freedom. For some Hindus, this is when your atman merges with Brahman.

# Texts and Teachings

## The Vedas

The earliest Hindu sacred texts are shruti texts called the Vedas. They date from the time of the Aryans, about 3500 years ago. They were not written down until centuries later, but were learned off by heart and passed on by word of mouth. The word Veda means 'knowledge'. Hindus believe that the Vedas were revealed directly by God, and that their teachings are eternal and cannot be changed. Verses from the Vedas are still used in Hindu worship, and also in many religious ceremonies (see pages 24-25).

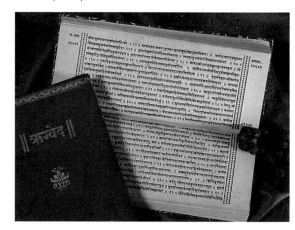

*A copy of the Rig Veda.*

The earliest Hindu sacred texts were composed in Sanskrit, the language of the Aryans. Sanskrit means 'perfected'. It is believed to be a sacred language with the power to communicate with the gods. But it is only effective if the priests are word-perfect when reciting the hymns. The script used to write Sanskrit is called devanagari, which means 'cities of the gods'.

## The four Vedas

There are four Vedas: the Rig Veda, Sama Veda, Yajur Veda and Atharva Veda. Each is a collection of hymns, prayers and instructions. The most sacred is the Rig Veda, or 'Song of Knowledge'. It contains 1028 hymns in praise of the gods who control the forces of nature. The Sama Veda contains melodies for singing the sacred hymns. The Yajur Veda gives instructions for priests. The Atharva Veda contains spells, chants and charms.

## Sacred fire

The Yajur Veda tells priests the correct way to perform rituals. The most important part of Aryan rituals was the havan, or sacred fire. The priest put offerings of butter, spices, grains and even animals, into the fire. The Aryans believed that Agni, god of fire, would carry the sacrifices to the gods, in return for the gods' blessing. The sacred fire is still used in Hindu ceremonies today (see page 24).

*A Hindu priest reciting from the sacred texts.*

## The story of creation

The Rig Veda contains many hymns about how the world was created. One tells of the sacrifice of Purusha, the first being, who had thousands of heads, eyes and feet. From his body, everything in the universe – the gods, Vedas, Moon and Sun, sky and earth, people and animals – were created.

"I praise Agni, the divine priest, who is the god of fire and sacrifice, the one who brings the gods' blessings. Agni is praised by all the wise men, past and present. May he bring the gods to this place."

(RIG VEDA)

# The Upanishads

The Upanishads are shruti texts which were composed about 2500 years ago. They take the form of teachings given by holy men, called gurus, to their pupils. The Sanskrit word Upanishad means 'to sit close by'. This is because the pupils traditionally sat at their gurus' feet to listen to them speak. The texts are also called Vedanta, which means 'the end of the Vedas', because they were composed at the end of the Vedic period. Like the Vedas, they were not written down until many centuries after they were first composed.

*Children studying at school, sitting near their teacher.*

> *" Just as a caterpillar reaches the tip of one blade of grass, then starts to crawl up another blade, so does atman leave one body behind and start its next life in another one, until it reaches Brahman."*
>
> (Brihadaranyaka Upanishad)

## Main Upanishads

There are more than 100 Upanishads but 13 of them are thought of as especially sacred. The longest (and oldest) of these are the Brihadaranyaka Upanishad and the Chandogya Upanishad, with hundreds of verses. The shortest is the Isa Upanishad, with only 18 verses.

## Basic teachings

The Upanishads explain the most important beliefs of Hinduism. They concentrate on the relationship between Brahman, the great soul, and atman, a person's individual soul, and how the two merge together to become one. They also talk about karma and the cycle of birth, death and rebirth. They teach that the way to achieve moksha, or freedom from rebirth, is by knowledge. You must get rid of ignorance and see things as they really are.

In Hinduism, gurus are holy teachers who devote their lives to teaching, meditation and studying the sacred texts. Gurus often have groups of followers who try to live according to the gurus' teachings because they believe that this will help them to achieve moksha. Many Hindus have a particular guru whom they ask for spiritual advice at difficult times in their lives.

## The story of the salt

The Upanishads often use stories to explain difficult messages and ideas. One story about the nature of Brahman comes from the Chandogya Upanishad. The story tells of a father who was teaching his son about Brahman. He told his son to put some salt into a bowl of water. The next day, he told him to take the salt out of the water again. Of course, this was impossible because the salt had dissolved. The lesson of the story was that just as the salt cannot be seen, but is in the water, so Brahman is invisible but is everywhere.

15

# The Ramayana

Ordinary Hindus do not usually read the shruti texts. It is the priests who study these texts, then explain their teachings and meanings. For most Hindus, the smriti texts are much more popular. These include two very long poems, called the Ramayana and the Mahabharata (see pages 18-19). Hindus honour and revere these texts, and try to live their lives according to the values and lessons they teach.

## The Original Ramayana

It is said that the Ramayana was composed in the 2nd century BCE by a wise man called Valmiki. Legend says that Rama

*A page from a copy of the Ramayana, showing Rama and Sita in the forest.*

visited Valmiki and told him his life's story. The poem is 24,000 verses long, arranged in seven books. Like the Vedas, it was not written down for hundreds of years. But professional storytellers learned it off by heart and travelled from village to village, reciting it.

## The story of the Ramayana

The Ramayana tells the story of Rama, prince of Ayodhya. Rama is banished to the forest for 14 years, with his wife, Sita, and his brother, Lakshman. One day, Sita is kidnapped by Ravana, the terrible, ten-headed demon king of Lanka. With the help of the monkey god, Hanuman, and his army, Rama kills Ravana and rescues Sita. They return home to Ayodhya to be crowned king and queen.

## What the Ramayana teaches

Rama is an avatar of Lord Vishnu and one of the best-loved gods of Hinduism (see page 11). The main lesson of the Ramayana is the struggle between good and evil forces, with good triumphing. But the poem also deals with important values and qualities, such as love, loyalty and duty. Rama accepts his banishment without question, putting duty above his own happiness. He is a brave warrior and a just king. For Hindus, Rama and Sita are an ideal husband and wife, loving and faithful to each other.

"Whoever reads or hears the Ramayana daily, all their sins will be washed away. Whoever recites the Ramayana will have rich gifts of cows and gold. He will have a long life, and be honoured in this world and the next."

(THE RAMAYANA)

The most famous version of the Ramayana was written by the poet, Tulsi Das, in the 1570s. It is called the Ram Charit Manas, or 'The Lake of Rama's Deeds'. It was not written in Sanskrit like the original poem but in a language called Hindi which is easier to understand. This helped to bring the story and teachings to people who did not know Sanskrit. Since then, the Ramayana has been translated into many different languages.

# The Mahabharata

The Mahabharata is the world's longest poem, with some 100,000 verses, divided into 18 books. It is thought to date from the 3rd or 2nd centuries BCE, and to have been composed by a wise man, called Vyasa. Legend says that Vyasa dictated the poem to the elephant-headed god, Ganesha, who broke off his tusk to write it down. In fact, it was probably composed by many different authors over a long period of time.

*Ganesha, the elephant-headed god.*

## The story of the Mahabharata

The Mahabharata tells of the war between two closely related royal families, the Kauravas and the Pandavas. Both want to rule the kingdom of Hastinapura, near Delhi, which rightfully belongs to the Pandavas. As the story unfolds, the Kauravas cheat the Pandavas out of their throne.

"You have the right to do your duty,
But you have no right to the fruits of your actions.
Whatever the results of your actions may be,
Do not think of yourself as the cause.
And never try to avoid doing your duty."

(THE BHAGAVAD GITA)

# The Bhagavad Gita

The most important, and widely read, part of the Mahabharata is called the Bhagavad Gita, or 'The Song of the Lord'. Set on the battlefield, it takes the form of a conversation between Arjuna, a Pandava prince, and his charioteer, the god, Krishna. Arjuna is filled with horror at the thought of killing his relations, the Kauravas, and tells Krishna that he does not want to fight. Krishna replies that Arjuna must ignore his own feelings and do his duty as a warrior. Arjuna follows Krishna's advice and leads his army into battle. The fighting lasts for 18 days, until the Kauravas are destroyed.

*Krishna and Arjuna ride into battle.*

# The message of the Gita

The Bhagavad Gita contains many of the key teachings of Hinduism. The main message is that everyone must do their duty, or dharma, without expecting anything in return. It is through unselfish action, and bhakti, or devotion to God, that people can reach moksha. For millions of Hindus, the Bhagavad Gita is a favourite text. Many people read a few verses of the Gita every day, and consult it for guidance, comfort and advice about life's problems.

Krishna, the hero of the Bhagavad Gita, is one of the most popular Hindu gods. Like Rama, he is an avatar of Lord Vishnu. All over India, many Hindus worship Krishna and his wife Radha. There are many stories about Krishna's childhood and his love of mischief (see pages 27).

*A verse from the Bhagavad Gita.*

# The Puranas

*Krishna killing the serpent Kaliya.*

The Puranas are smriti texts, probably compiled between about 500 CE and 1500 CE. The word Purana is Sanskrit for 'ancient'. The Puranas are collections of myths and stories about the creation of the world, and the lives and adventures of the gods. The Puranas are very popular texts for Hindus because they teach them about the gods. Prayers from the Puranas are used in puja, or worship, and passages are recited in the mandir at festival times.

## The great Puranas

There are 18 maha, or great, Puranas, and many upa, or lesser, ones. The earlier Maha-Puranas contain a mixture of stories about different gods. The later Maha-Puranas tend to be dedicated to one god, such as Shiva, Vishnu or Krishna. The stories in the Puranas were written in the form of conversations, often between wise men or animals. Today, they are recited by special readers, called bhat.

## The Bhagavat Purana

The most popular of all the Puranas is the Bhagavat Purana. Dating from about the 10th century CE, it is divided into 12 volumes which praise and glorify Lord Vishnu and his avatars. The tenth book is the most widely read. It tells the story of Krishna's early life when he lived as a cowherd. One famous story tells how Krishna killed an evil serpent, Kaliya, which was poisoning the river near the village where Krishna lived.

## Stories of Ganesha

Ganesha, the son of Lord Shiva and his wife the goddess Parvati, is the Hindu god of wisdom and good fortune. Hindus pray to Ganesha before starting a journey or any new task. There are many stories in the Puranas about how Ganesha got his elephant head. One tells how Shiva chopped his son's head off in a temper. Filled with remorse, he promised to replace it with the head of the first animal he saw – which was an elephant.

*Part of a Purana text about Ganesha.*

Hindus believe that, from time to time, Lord Vishnu comes down to Earth to save the world from evil or disaster. Each descent is called an avatar. Nine out of ten avatars have already appeared on Earth. They include the most important avatars, the gods, Rama and Krishna. The tenth avatar, Kalki, a rider on a white horse, is still to come.

"Worship Shiva and his name will cleanse you of all your sins. You need not study the Vedas or the other holy books. You need not go on a pilgrimage. You need not practise yoga. You need not fear evil and even death itself need not frighten you." (SKANDA PURANA)

## Daily worship

Many Hindus read and listen to the sacred texts in their daily lives. They use them for spiritual guidance and practical advice. Verses from the Vedas and Puranas are recited as daily prayers. Myths and stories help Hindus to understand their religion better. The sacred texts are treated with great respect. They are often placed on a shrine, wrapped in silk cloths. They are never put directly on the floor, nor touched with dirty hands. Prayers are often recited before reading from them.

## Hindu puja

Hindu worship is called puja. Many Hindus set aside a quiet place as a shrine, with murtis (sacred images) or pictures of their favourite gods. Here they perform puja every morning and evening. They say prayers and recite verses from the sacred texts. They also make offerings of flowers, fruit and sweets to the gods, in return for the gods' blessings. Some Hindus start each day with a prayer to the Sun. It comes from the Rig Veda and is called the Gayatri Mantra.

*Making an offering to the gods in the mandir.*

"Aum. We meditate on the brilliant light and great glory of the divine Sun. May it guide our minds and inspire us." (GAYATRI MANTRA: RIG VEDA)

*Early morning puja by the River Ganges.*

The word 'Aum' is chanted at the beginning and end of prayers and readings from the sacred texts, as instructed in the Manusmriti. For Hindus, aum is the most sacred word and symbol. It is made up of three sounds which separately represent Brahma, Vishnu and Shiva, and together represent Brahman.

## Priests and texts

Many Hindus also worship in the mandir, or temple. This worship is supervised by a Brahmin, or priest. Hindu priests spend many years learning Sanskrit and studying the sacred texts. They learn large parts of the texts off by heart. Many Hindus cannot read Sanskrit. Instead, they listen to the priests reciting from the texts. The priests also give sermons and talks to explain the teachings of the texts. There are special schools of recitation of the Vedic texts in southern India. Priests teach the texts to children who learn to recite them. The recitation is accompanied by different hand gestures.

## The laws of Manu

Rules for how Hindus should live and worship are found in an ancient Sanskrit text, called the Manusmriti, or The Laws of Manu (see page 6). It is one of a group of texts called the Dharmshastras, or law books, and was written in about 300 CE. It includes rules for reciting the Vedas, a code of behaviour for each stage of life, and guidance for kings, gurus and priests.

*The sacred Aum symbol.*

# Times of life

In Hinduism, key times in a person's life are traditionally marked by ceremonies, called samskaras. These ceremonies are set out in the sacred texts (see box). Each ceremony takes place in front of a sacred fire and is conducted by a priest, who performs the rituals and recites verses from the sacred texts. The priest also explains the ceremony to the people taking part and guides them through the different steps.

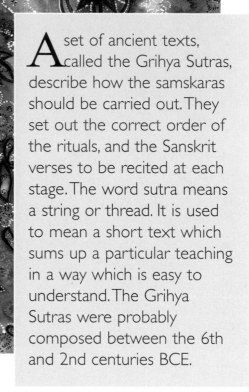

A set of ancient texts, called the Grihya Sutras, describe how the samskaras should be carried out. They set out the correct order of the rituals, and the Sanskrit verses to be recited at each stage. The word sutra means a string or thread. It is used to mean a short text which sums up a particular teaching in a way which is easy to understand. The Grihya Sutras were probably composed between the 6th and 2nd centuries BCE.

*A Hindu boy with his sacred thread.*

## Sacred thread

When a Hindu boy is about 10 years old, he receives his sacred thread from the priest. This ceremony marks the start of the boy's adult and religious life. He promises to study the sacred texts and to follow the rules of the Manusmriti. He is also taught to recite the Gayatri Mantra by his father (see page 22). In the past, boys left home to live with their guru and complete their studies.

## Wedding days

A Hindu wedding lasts for several days, with 15 different rituals to perform on the wedding day itself. The priest guides the bride and groom through the ceremony and recites verses from the sacred texts for them to repeat. The most important part of the ceremony is when the couple take seven steps around the sacred fire. At each step, they make a vow for food, health, wealth, happiness, children, strength and lifelong friendship.

*A Hindu wedding around the sacred fire.*

"May your sight return to the Sun, And your life's breath return to the wind. May your soul go to the sky or mingle with the oceans, or once more return to Earth, depending on your actions." (RIG VEDA)

## A Hindu funeral

When a Hindu dies, his or her body is taken for cremation. While the person's eldest son or male relation lights the funeral pyre, the priest recites verses from the Vedas, such as the one below. The verses remind mourners that the soul never dies but is reborn until it finally achieves moksha. Verses from the Bhagavad Gita may also be read, to comfort the mourners.

# Hindu festivals

There are hundreds of Hindu festivals throughout the year. Many are linked to stories from the sacred texts which tell of the gods' birthdays and other special events in their lives. Celebrations include reading or listening to the stories, or seeing them acted out in plays and dances.

*The Kecak (Monkey Dance) is performed to tell a story from the Ramayana.*

## Stories of Rama

Several festivals are based on stories from the Ramayana. In September, Hindus remember Rama's victory over Ravana at the festival of Dassehra. The story is retold in a play, called the Rama Lila. The festival of Diwali is celebrated in October or November. People decorate their homes and mandir with tiny lamps, called divas. These are meant to welcome Rama and Sita home, after their long years in exile.

Stories from the sacred texts are very important for teaching Hindu children about their religion. They are told in many different ways, through film, drama and dance. Children can read them in comic books, and even watch them on TV. In India, a recent television series of the Ramayana was so popular that extra episodes had to be added on to the end.

## Krishna's birthday

In August or September, Hindus celebrate the festival of Janmashtami, Krishna's birthday. In the mandir dedicated to Krishna, the priests read out the story of Krishna's birth from the Bhagavata Purana. The story tells how, when Krishna was born, his wicked uncle, King Kamsa, wanted to kill him. But Krishna's father, Vasudeva, secretly carried him across the river to the village of Vrindavan. Here Krishna was brought up in safety by a cowherd and his wife.

*People dressed up for the Rama Lila.*

"When Lord Krishna was about to be born, kettledrums sounded in heaven, the heavenly musicians sang and the spirits danced for joy. Wise men and gods showered down flowers, and clouds gently rumbled like ocean waves."

(BHAGAVATA PURANA)

## Durga Puja

Durga is the fierce-looking Hindu goddess of war. She is shown, dressed for battle, riding on a lion or tiger. At the festival of Durga Puja, in September or October, Hindus remember a story about Durga from the Markandeya Purana. It tells how Durga killed the evil demon, Mahish, who was disguised as a giant buffalo. Legend said that he could not be killed, except by a woman.

**Aryan** According to some scholars, a nomadic people from Central Asia who arrived in India from about 1500 BCE.

**Atharva Veda** The fourth of the Vedas. It contains chants, charms and hymns of praise.

**Atman** A person's individual soul which may be born again and again in different bodies.

**Aum** The most sacred Hindu word and sound. It represents God and all creation.

**Avatar** The 'descent' of a god to Earth in a different form. The best-known avatars are those of Vishnu.

**Bhagavad Gita** The Song of the Lord. It is part of the Mahabharata, spoken by Krishna. For many Hindus, it is the most sacred text.

**Bhagavata Purana** One of the collection of sacred texts, called the Puranas. It praises Vishnu and his avatars.

**Bhakti** Loving devotion to God.

**Bhakti yoga** The path of loving devotion to God. One of the paths for reaching moksha.

**Bhat** Special scholars who recite the Puranas.

**Brahma** One of the three main gods of Hinduism. He is the creator of the universe.

**Brahman** The great soul, or spirit, sometimes called God, which is the invisible but eternal force behind all existence.

**Devanagari** The script in which Sanskrit is written. It means 'cities of the gods'.

**Dharma** Law or teaching. For Hindus, it means doing their duty towards their family and friends.

**Dharmshastras** A group of Hindu law books which set out rules for living and worshipping.

**Diva** A small clay lamp, filled with oil, which is lit on the festival of Divali.

**Durga** The Hindu mother goddess in her fierce form. Durga is the goddess of war.

**Ganesha** The elephant-headed god. Hindus believe that he removes obstacles and worship him before any new task.

**Grihya Sutras** A set of texts which give instructions for how the samskaras should be carried out.

**Guru** A religious teacher.

**Havan** The sacred fire which is the focus of Hindu sacred rituals and ceremonies.

**Hindi** A modern Indian language.

**Jnana yoga** The path of knowledge and study of the sacred texts. One of the paths for reaching moksha.

**Karma** The law of cause and effect. How the quality of your actions in this life affects how you will be reborn.

**Karma yoga** The path of good, selfless action. One of the paths for reaching moksha.

**Krishna** One of the avatars of Vishnu and one of the most popular Hindu gods. His teachings are found in the Bhagavad Gita.

**Mahabharata** The epic poem which tells the story of the battle between the Kaurava and Pandava princes.

**Mandir** A Hindu temple.

**Manusmriti** The Laws of Manu. An ancient text which gives laws for living and worshipping.

**Markandeya Purana** One of the great Puranas which contains the story of Durga killing the demon, Mahish.

**Moksha** Freedom or salvation for the soul when it breaks free of the cycle of birth and rebirth.

**Murtis** Sacred images which represent the gods and goddesses and are used as a focus of worship.

**Puja** Hindu worship at home or in the mandir.

**Puranas** A collection of sacred texts which contain myths and stories about creation, and about the gods.

**Raja yoga** The path of yoga and meditation. One of the paths for reaching moksha.

**Ram Charit Manas** A very popular version of the Ramayana, written in the 1570s by the poet, Tulsi Das.

**Rama** One of the avatars of Vishnu and one of the most popular Hindu gods. His story is told in the Ramayana.

**Ramayana** The epic poem which tells the story of Rama, and his wife, Sita. One of the best loved Hindu sacred texts.

**Rig Veda** The Song of Knowledge. The earliest Hindu scripture which contains hundreds of hymns in praise of the gods.

**Sama Veda** The second of the Vedas. It gives instructions and melodies for chanting the sacred hymns.

**Samsara** The cycle of birth, death and rebirth in which everyone is caught up, until they achieve moksha.

**Samskara** Ceremonies performed at important times in a Hindu's life, such as at birth, on getting married and on death.

**Sanatana dharma** Eternal teaching. This is what Hindus call their set of religious beliefs.

**Sanskrit** An ancient Indian language and the sacred language of the Hindu scriptures.

**Shakti** Energy or power, especially of a Hindu goddess.

**Shiva** One of the three main gods of Hinduism. He is the destroyer of evil in the universe.

**Shruti** That which is heard. A term which means the Vedas and the Upanishads.

**Sita** The wife of Rama.

**Smriti** That which is remembered. A term which means the Ramayana, the Mahabharata and the Puranas.

**Sutra** A short verse or saying from a sacred text.

**Upanishads** Sacred texts based on the teachings of a guru to his disciple. Also called Vedanta, or the end of the Vedas.

**Vedas** Four collections of hymns, prayers and instructions. The earliest Hindu sacred texts.

**Vedic period** The period of history in which the Vedas were composed.

**Vishnu** One of the three main gods of Hinduism. He is the protector and preserver of the universe.

**Yajur Veda** The third of the Vedas. It contains instructions for priests for performing rituals.

# Index